The Catholic Mother's Resource Guide

by

Maria Compton-Hernandez

The Catholic Mother's Resource Guide:

A Resource Listing of Hints and Ideas for Practicing and Teaching the Faith

by
Maria Compton-Hernandez

Published by:

The Riehle Foundation
P.O. Box 7
Milford, OH 45150 USA
513-576-0032

Published by The Riehle Foundation
For additional copies, write:

The Riehle Foundation
P.O. Box 7
Milford, OH 45150 - 0007 USA
513-576-0032

Updated edition September, 1998

Library of Congress Catalog Card No: 96-70666

ISBN: 1-877678-44-9

Table of Contents

Dedication

To my mother, who taught me most of the hints and ideas in this booklet, and to my dear Blessed Mother, who brought me back to her Son. Also, to Michael, my husband, and my most precious children: Corbin, Emilee, Shelbee, Mary-Therese, Catherine Anne, and Grace.

Introduction

The purpose of this little booklet is to help other Catholic mothers in their quest to raise their children in the beauty and truths of the Roman Catholic Faith. It is also intended as a way to help Catholic mothers find time in their busy, often hectic lives to develop and grow in their own spiritual lives within our Church. The ideas and examples, as well as a helpful resource list, are included in a way that makes them concrete and easy to implement. I currently have six children, ages 10, 9, 7, 4, 2 1/2 and 8 months. The concept of this book came to me in a bout of insomnia which accompanied me in the latter part of my fifth pregnancy. All of the ideas, activities and suggestions have been "field tested" and mother approved! The booklet is divided into two sections: Part 1 deals with ideas and hints which will help industrious moms find simple ways to grow in their own prayer lives. Part 2 gives hints and simple activities which mothers can use to pass on the beautiful, rich traditions of our Roman Catholic Faith and heritage to our most precious gifts — our children. The concepts in both sections are simple and meant to be a source list which moms can browse through, choose, and try out on their own.

PART I

A BUSY MOM'S GUIDE TO DEVELOPING A PRACTICAL PRAYER LIFE AMONG THE DAILY DEMANDS OF MOTHERHOOD

I used to think that in order to have a real spiritual life, I had to say a set number of prayers, chaplets, Scripture reading or other devotionals every day. As my family grew, I found it impossible to keep up with the rigorous demands of such a prayer life—how am I supposed to sit down and read from this prayer book when I have three loads of laundry to do, a floor to mop, a baby to nurse, and a list of errands to run? It was my own mother who helped me to see that my prayer life can be incorporated into the busy demands of a mother, and that, indeed, my vocation of motherhood can in *itself* be offered up as one continuous prayer. The list of hints in this section are practices that I have been taught by my own mom, as well as others that I have just stumbled upon myself. I hope you may find some of them helpful.

Develop a real relationship with the Blessed Mother

This is one of the most important ways mothers can truly become close to Our Lord. Developing a strong dependence upon the Blessed Mother is truly the first step of worshipping her Son. No one better understands the demands of a mother than she who was the most perfect mother of all. Our Lady was an unwed mother at the time she conceived; the mother of Jesus as a baby, a teenager, and a young man. She experienced the same joys and sorrows of all mothers — she was even a single mother for a while, a widow, and finally, a mother who watched the cruel death of her only Son. My own journey back into the Roman Catholic Church (after being a "cafeteria Catholic" for many years) started with a renewed devotion to Our Lady.

One of the finest and best prayers a mother can say to please Our Lord is the Rosary. The busy activities of a mother's day allow time in which the various decades of the Rosary can be said. Don't start off trying to say all 15 decades at once. Begin with one decade if you have never said a Rosary before. Over time, work your way up to a five-decade Rosary. (I was at this stage for several years!) Eventually, you'll find that there are ample opportunities throughout your day to say all 15 decades – although not all in one sitting. That's the beauty of the Rosary. It is divided into decades which are small and doable. The Rosary is a wonderful reflection on the life of Christ, especially if you can do all 15 decades at different points throughout your day. On most days I am able to get all 15 decades of my Rosary said; even on the most hectic days I will always find a few minutes to say at least 5 decades.

Here's how I do it: take advantage of any opportunity which is fairly quiet to say as many decades as you can. Most moms I know have found that one of the best places to pray the Rosary is while driving. Keep a rosary in your car for this occasion, or wear a rosary ring. I found one way to help me keep track of which decade I'm on while getting in and out of the car is to have a rosary meditation booklet in the car which has good pictures (Resource 1). I keep the booklet open to the picture which corresponds to the decade I am saying. That way I always know which decade I'm praying. Other moms I spoke with use rosary tapes to listen to the Rosary; there are a variety of such tapes available at any Catholic bookstore.

You may not be able to say all of the Rosary while driving, so look for other good opportunities for quiet time throughout your day to do it. Another time I find is when I go for a daily walk (either outside or on a treadmill in our home). Walking the kids to the park, waiting through a long soccer practice and other such opportunites can also be used. We also keep rosaries strategically placed throughout our home, so that at any given free moment (rocking the baby to sleep, kids' study time) I can grab a rosary and pray parts of it as time allows. When praying your daily Rosary becomes a habit, you may find more and more of these opportunities to pray the mysteries of the Rosary throughout your entire day.

Memorize indulgenced prayers and say them often throughout your day

I found a great way to pray is to choose highly indulgenced prayers and get into the habit of saying them often. (For an explanation of indulgences, see Appendix B.) Here is a great hint for doing this: place a particular prayer you'd like to memorize on your fridge. Every time you pass by it throughout your busy day, stop to read the prayer. After a few days of this, you'll have the prayer memorized. Another way is to place prayers you'd like to say daily on your bathroom mirror. One prayer that is especially important to say every morning is a consecration prayer for your family, naming each child and your husband. There are many consecration prayers available in a variety of prayer books, so pick one and paste it on your mirror. Eventually, you will find that reading the prayers daily will allow you to memorize them.

Once you have a few selected prayers memorized, you can say them anytime throughout your day, even when your hands are full of laundry baskets or crying infants. Not all indulgenced prayers are long – just saying prayerfully the name of Jesus is a wonderful prayer (see Resource 2). Good times to squeeze in these memorized prayers are, for example, every time you go up and down a flight of stairs, as you are folding laundry, while filling your gas tank...the opportunities are endless! Another time which may seem silly, but always works for me, is in the morning while I shower. I have three prayers I like to say daily, and I find the quiet of the shower is a great time to say them every morning.

Start with just a few memorized favorite prayers. As time goes on, you'll find you are able to memorize more and more. The key to remember is: you don't have to sit down with a prayer book or Bible to pray!

Take advantage of any opportunity to pray

It may seem obvious, but there are plenty of times during your day and night when you could be praying which may have never occurred to you. When you wake up at night with insomnia or to tend to a crying baby, don't see it as a loss of sleep. View it instead as an opportunity to pray. You're up anyway!

Make night prayers brief and meaningful

It's important to end your day on a prayerful note, but don't take on a nighttime prayer regimen that is too demanding for you. Pick one or two simple, short memorized prayers to say as you climb into bed. Choose a single prayer or brief meditation from a bedside book to read or on which to meditate. Offer every beat of your heart as a prayer while you sleep — then you've got your whole night covered!

Do a simple nightly examination of conscience

One great method another mom taught me which I continue to use is the desolation/ consolation examination. It's very quick and you can do it before you drift off to sleep. You simply meditate on the events of the day and ask yourself, "What gave me desolation today?" What made you feel bad, lose your temper, become angry or resentful, or just generally made you feel unhappy? Try to focus on one event and offer it to Our Lord, asking for His help and guidance on how you can improve/change that situation and perhaps prevent it from happening again. Next ask yourself, "What gave me consolation today?" What made you feel happy, satisfied, joyful, spiritually uplifted, or just made you smile? Thank God for this event and pray for the person(s) involved in the episode.

Offer up the mundane duties of motherhood as a prayer

Let's face it — the vocation of motherhood is not glamorous. Much of the time is spent doing ordinary duties...changing diapers, grocery shopping, putting away laundry. Take the duties that are the most distasteful to you (mine's laundry!) and offer the act itself up to Jesus as a prayer. Remember that the Blessed Mother and St. Joseph performed these same ordinary duties around the home in Bethlehem. I try to envision that the dirty laundry in the basket I'm carrying is Jesus' laundry, and He's come to ask me to do it for Him...somehow it makes it a little easier to do! Remember, even the smallest acts of motherhood can become a prayer if they are offered up in such a spirit.

Turn off the soaps!

Many moms like to have soap operas on during the day, if only to listen to while working around the house. These are a distraction and most will admit the content is not really something you want to have on in a Christian home. As a former soap opera addict (*The Young and the Restless*!), I found the day I made the difficult decision to turn off the soaps for good was the day my prayer life took a permanent turn for the better.

Go to Eucharistic Adoration for at least an hour a week if possible

I will admit, I didn't even know what Eucharistic Adoration was a few years ago, but now my weekly holy hour has become an important cornerstone of my faith. A lot of churches today offer Perpetual Eucharistic Adoration (24 hours a day, every day of the year, Our Lord in the Blessed Sacrament is exposed on the altar for all to visit and adore). Many other churches offer at least a few set hours a week for Eucharistic Adoration. Our church did not offer any weekly opportunities for this, so we approached the pastor and asked. Sometimes asking is all that's needed and a pastor will be happy to provide regular opportunities for Eucharistic Adoration for your parish. We started with just three hours one evening a week, and now have an additional three hours every Monday – Friday mornings. Hopefully, this will expand to Perpetual Eucharistic Adoration as more parishioners find out about this wonderful way to pray.

The great thing about Eucharistic Adoration which most busy moms appreciate is the TOTAL SILENCE! It is a time of complete quiet and prayerful encounter with Our Lord in the Blessed Sacrament. There are no specific prayers you must say during a holy hour. You can bring any variety of spiritual writings, Scripture and meditation books to guide you (see Resource 3). Or you can just sit there and enjoy the silence as you visit quietly with Our Lord. Once you begin the practice of establishing a weekly holy hour, you will become hooked and will cherish this solitude as a prayerful break in your hectic week.

Keep blessed objects and holy pictures throughout your home

Anyone who comes into your house should be able to find something to tell them that you are a Roman Catholic. Keeping crucifixes and pictures of the Holy Family and various saints throughout your home is a visual reminder of our faith. Seeing them as you go about the duties of your day will help to spur you on to simple prayers from the heart and will bring your thoughts back to God, if only for a moment. Keeping blessed objects like holy medals and blessed holy cards around your house will also serve as powerful spiritual protection for your home.

You can obtain a large supply of free blessed Miraculous Medals (see Resource 4) and place one above each doorway of your home. You can also bury them in the property outside of your home. St. Benedict medals (available through any Catholic Bookstore or see Appendix A), are also recommended to place above doorways for protection against evil. The best thing to do is to have a priest come and bless your home or do an enthronement of your home to the Sacred and Immaculate Hearts. These practices, when done in total faith and not superstition, will keep your home safer than any home security system on the market! For a complete listing of sacramentals for your home, see Appendix A.

Keep holy water around and use it in abundance

The spiritual treasure of holy water and its powerful protection over evil are well documented in the Catholic Church. Keep an abundant supply of holy water around and don't be afraid to use it. When children are small, teach them the wonders of holy water. We put holy water in a spray squirt bottle (marked clearly) and used it to douse the kids' rooms every night before bedtime to keep away bad dreams, and any other evil or harm, real or imagined. Put holy water founts in prominent places in your home and try to keep them filled. Encourage your kids to use it often throughout the day when they pass by and before going to bed. You obtain a release from venial sin every time you use holy water, so make use of it yourself throughout the day as you think of it. Keep a small bottle of holy water in your car and bless your vehicle occasionally, especially before traveling on a long journey. For information on acquiring holy water, see Appendix A.

House Blessing

Having your home blessed by a priest is another added grace. If your priest is unavailable, you could obtain holy water from your church and you and your family could bless your home together. The blessing may begin by walking together through your home saying a short prayer while sprinkling a little holy water in each room and around your property, see Resourse 5.

When you go on vacation, don't leave your faith at home

There are many beautiful old Roman Catholic Churches and shrines scattered throughout the United States. Some are just off major highways. Check out a road map before traveling, or obtain a list of shrines by calling the United States Catholic Conference, 1-800-235-USCC and ask for their free publication *Catholic Shrines and Places of Pilgrimage*. Build a few extra minutes into your traveling schedule to stop and see some of these beautiful storehouses of Catholic treasure and tradition. The Church extends a special blessing to all pilgrims who visit Shrines.

Try Contemporary Christian Music

If you're a fan of oldies, pop, or rock, turn the radio dial to the nearest Contemporary Christian Music station. You'll be surprised how enjoyable CCM music is to listen to, and the lyrics are often a prayer in itself. Keep CCM music on in the car for your children to hear; they'll never know it's not the regular rock station!

Invest in and keep a library of good Catholic literature in your home

This is something that you can invest in and acquire over time, and will be an invaluable resource for you to have. Some staples you'll want to procure for your own library may include: 1) a traditional Catholic Bible – beware of some of the newer translations. Stick to the good old standby Catholic Bibles, like the Douay Rheims version; 2) a copy of the *Catechism of the Catholic Church* – this is now available in hardback, soft cover, and a smaller paperback version and is an invaluable resource for any Catholic home; 3) books about the lives of the saints; 4) a variety of prayer and meditation books; and 5) defending the faith books (see Resource 6) – books written to help Roman Catholics defend their faith to those who question things like the Pope, devotion to the Blessed Mother, the Eucharist, etc. (see Additional Resources).

Start or join a prayer group for mothers within your parish

When several of the mothers of our parish were touched and deeply converted by the book *The Apostolate of Holy Motherhood* (see Resource 7), we decided to approach our pastor and ask permission to start a weekly prayer group. We keep the guidelines loose and simple: come any Sunday evening you are free, and pray! The format of the prayer group sessions is about an hour long – short Stations of the Cross, the Rosary, selected other prayers read together from a manual we put together, and open discussion about topics related to our faith and motherhood. Bonding with other mothers who share your commitment to the Catholic faith is a great spiritual boost and a wonderful way to make lasting friendships.

Get a computer and learn about using the Internet

The Internet, or World Wide Web (WWW) is a doorway to any information that is available on the information superhighway. There are huge sections on the WWW devoted to Roman Catholicism which you can access from your home computer. The sections include encyclicals of the popes, lives of the saints, Scripture, information about religious orders, doctrines and dogmas of our faith. Virtually anything you could ever want or need related to our faith can now be found on the WWW. It's like having access to every Catholic library in the world at your fingertips. If you aren't able to purchase a computer yourself, many libraries and college university campus computer centers allow the public to sign up to use their computers.

You can also purchase the *Catechism of the Catholic Church* in a computerized version especially geared to teaching young children (see Resource 8). Computer use and using the

WWW, like television, needs to be carefully monitored. There is a plethora of wonderful material on the WWW, but there is also a lot of junk. If you already have a computer with the capacity to be on the WWW, for the great places to visit regarding Roman Catholicism, see Resource 9.

Establish a visible sign of your faith for all to see

Ours is a beautiful statue of the Blessed Mother which we put in a prominent place in our front yard. Each year, around May Day, we plant a new flower garden and dedicate it to Our Lady. You can also place a cross on or above your front doorway, or buy a door knocker that is a sign of your Catholic Faith. Don't be afraid to let the world know you are Roman Catholic and proud of it!

Keep spiritual literature in your car

I keep a variety of prayer books (like the *Pieta* prayer book, and *The Apostolate of Holy Motherhood* book) in my van. You never know when you may be stuck at an extra long soccer practice or waiting in a long drive-through line and could pick it up for a quick read. Also, they can serve as handy evangelization tools if you meet someone who may be interested in learning more about our faith.

Bless your children before bedtime

Go in and trace a Sign of the Cross on your children's foreheads when you tuck them into bed. Say a short, spontaneous prayer asking for blessings to be upon them while they sleep. This is a good time to say a quick prayer to your children's guardian angels and to entrust them into the angels' care for the night.

Get a shortwave radio for WEWN or cable television for EWTN

If your local cable company doesn't carry EWTN (the Eternal Word Television Network by Mother Angelica), buy a short-wave radio and get the same wonderful orthodox Catholic programming by WEWN This radio station by Mother Angelica carries quality Catholic programming 24 hours a day. Keep it in the kitchen, or whichever room you are in the most, and leave it on while you do household chores. Short-wave radios cost around $100 for the small version, or $150 - $200 for the larger, fancier version with built-in cassette. It is an investment that is worth every penny.

Go to Marian conferences and Catholic workshops

If possible, do this with your spouse. Marian Conferences are like a pep rally for your faith. They provide an opportunity to be totally immersed in basic themes related to our faith and are usually packed into a weekend format. The conferences that my husband and I have attended together have been mostly out of town, so we had to save a bit in order to go. But they provide a wonderful opportunity for time away from the kids, and they spiritually bring us closer together. If it's not possible for both of you to attend together, take turns going to them. They provide an excellent chance for spiritual renewal and a way to make contacts with other Catholics who cherish their faith as much as you do. Franciscan University in Steubenville, Ohio, offers a variety of courses and workshops for both youth and adults, as well as some for the entire family.

Do the Total Consecration of yourself and your family to the Immaculate Heart of Mary

The ideal consecration format is the one developed by St. Louis de Montfort (see Resource 10). This consecration to Our Lady is a set of prayers said over a period of time in which you totally give yourself and all you possess to Our Lady. If you can get your husband to do the consecration with you, that's even better. Any child old enough to read and understand the prayers may also be included. When you do the consecration, you will notice a spiritual renewal in your own prayer life. It will bring your relationship with the Blessed Mother to new heights. After you have completed the consecration, buy a simple silver chain to wear around your wrist all the time in memory of this blessed event. My consecration chain is endless, without a clasp, so that I never take it off. I am reminded to say quick and simple prayers to the Blessed Mother throughout my day whenever I happen to look at it.

Wear a brown scapular

This is something that Our Lady has been asking since she appeared at Fatima, yet very few post Vatican II Catholics wear them today. Our Lady has mentioned the need to return to this practice in many modern day apparitions. A scapular is hard to wear in the beginning, but with a few prayers for fortitude and a little perseverance, you will become so accustomed to it that you will notice immediately when you forget to put it on. It is a powerful sacramental of the Church, with wonderful promises attached to it for spiritual and temporal safety. Wearing one is truly being wrapped in the mantle of Our Lady. There is also a green scapular (should not replace the brown one) which may be carried, put under a pillow, or placed in your home. The green scapular is known for healing and conversion.

Be aware and informed of social and political issues

The best way to do this is to listen to the Christian News Radio station or watch the Christian news on the local Christian TV station, along with the regular nightly news broadcasts from the secular media. There is a lot of news which the secular press simply chooses to ignore that Christian stations are not afraid to cover. To be good parents, we need to be informed and aware of what's going on in our world today. There are lots of Catholic magazines, newspapers and periodicals which can help you keep abreast of the major issues (see Appendix D).

Explore your faith regarding any personal unanswered questions

If there is a doctrine of our faith which has you confused or unsure, explore it and find out why our Church teaches this particular aspect. When we were first married, I did not understand the Church's stand on birth control, so I assumed that my own confusion meant that I was not bound to follow this doctrine of my faith. As time went on, I was led to read the encyclical *Humane Vitae,* by Pope Paul VI, which defines this particular teaching in a way that is simple to understand and truly beautiful. I went on my own quest of reading and study to find the answer, and found that the Catholic Church was right all along.

Don't let your own misunderstanding of a doctrine of our faith cause you to be in error. Women priests, the Eucharist, papal infallibility, —whatever the issue may be that is causing you concern or doubts — simply explore it! Read voraciously anything that will help you to clarify the Church's stand on a particular issue. Seek spiritual guidance from a good, traditional priest as well. Another great source is a magazine called *Catholic Answers* (see Appendix D). You can be assured that the Catholic Church truly has THE ANSWER to any doubts or questions — but you may need to go on your own spiritual quest to find it!

Don't overload on a set of daily required prayers

As I began my faith journey in earnest several years ago, I kept running across wonderful prayers, chaplets, and devotions which had terrific promises attached to all who would say them. It seemed like each week I was adding a new litany, prayer, or novena that I felt like I had to say every day. Pretty soon I was simply overloaded. The prayers became something I HAD to do, and I began finding very little spiritual joy in them. This led to feeling scrupulous about them and experiencing feelings of guilt if I did not "get them all in" before bedtime. It finally dawned on me that I could never do all the prayers in the world that have indulgences and wonderful promises attached. It was crazy and impossible to try, and I was left feeling spiritually arid.

I chose a few prayers that I determined were basic and critical to a healthy daily prayer life. The ones I decided upon were the Rosary and the Chaplet of Divine Mercy (see Resource 11). These I found I could do nearly every day. The rest of the prayers could be said on an occasional basis as needed. I felt like the weight of the world was lifted off my shoulders! What a joy not to feel bound by having to say a set number of prayers every day. It is just as spiritually enriching to say spontaneous prayers from the heart and simple memorized prayers throughout my busy day. All of these, in union with the duties and sacrifices of being a mother, are wonderful prayers to be offered to Our Dear Lord.

Conclusion

Some of these simple activities and ideas may seem obvious, but I acquired them over a period of several years. I've often thought that it would have been nice to have a list of these ideas when I first began my faith journey as a mother, instead of stumbling across them over time as I did. I hope that perhaps you've found one or two that you may incorporate into your own life as a mother to help you to grow spiritually closer to Our Lord and His Blessed Mother.

PART II

A MOTHER'S GUIDE TO TEACHING THE RICHES AND TRADITIONS OF THE ROMAN CATHOLIC FAITH TO HER CHILDREN

Preface: Now let's explore some simple, concrete ways that Catholic mothers can teach the faith to their children.

Establish a family altar and nightly prayer routine

Find a place in your home where you can set up a small family altar. Children, especially young ones, like to see, hear, smell and touch their faith. Put a blessed candle on your altar, along with a small holy water font if possible. Add statues or pictures of the Sacred Heart and Immaculate Heart, and any other saints of special devotion. Gather around the altar to do nightly family prayers whenever possible. Light the candle (my kids love to turn off all the lights!), and try to involve each child individually. We let each child take a turn leading a **Hail Mary** while the rest respond. Choose a set of prayers which you can say nightly, and even the youngest children will soon have them memorized. Some ideas for nighttime prayers include: the **Hail Mary** (perhaps do a decade or a full family Rosary if your kids are old enough); the **Our Father**, the **Glory Be**, the **Guardian Angel Prayer**, **St. Michael the Archangel Prayer**, and the Fatima prayers (see Prayer List). Younger kids can take turns blowing out the candle after prayers are recited. Allow everyone to bless themselves with holy water before going to bed. Through such simple things as holy water and blessed candles, the younger children can truly experience in a physical sense the rich beauties of our faith.

Teach your children everyday opportunities for prayer

There are countless daily opportunities to teach children to pray. One example is saying a quick prayer and doing the Sign of the Cross whenever you drive past a Catholic Church. This acknowledges to the children the True Presence of Our Lord in the Eucharist in the Tabernacle. You can say little prayers like, "Jesus, I love you," or, "Jesus, Mary, Joseph, I love you, save souls." Teach children to say a simple prayer for the holy souls in Purgatory whenever you pass by a graveyard. Another practice to benefit the holy souls is to allow the children to sprinkle holy water while saying a quick prayer on their behalf whenever the children go to bless themselves with holy water. Every time you pass by a house with a garden statue of the Blessed Mother or Our Lord, teach the children to say a quick prayer. Whenever an ambulance passes by or is heard in the distance, teach the children to say a **Hail Mary** or prayer from the heart for the person who may be in danger of death. Another wonderful habit is to teach your children how to make reparation against blasphemies committed against the name of God and the holy name of Jesus. Clarify with your children about what it means to use the name of God or the name of Jesus in vain. Then, teach them to make reparation whenever they hear someone else do so by saying simply, "Blessed be God's holy name," or, "Blessed be the name of Jesus."

When you go to Mass, bring the children and sit in the front of the church

Cryrooms and children's baby-sitting options for parents make it tempting to avoid bringing the little ones into church. There may be a period of time when it is truly impossible to bring them in (i.e., crawling age to about age two is a killer!). But, when possible, try to bring children into church. Cryrooms are sometimes a necessity, but often are overloaded and filled with toys. This creates a circus atmosphere and does not teach reverence for the Mass.

When children are old enough to understand correction, start bringing them into the church and sit together as a family. The best place for little ones to sit is the front row (which you'll find almost always is the last to fill up!). The closer the children are to the Mass, the more the sights and sounds of the Eucharistic Celebration become real to them. When they can see what's going on, they are less likely to act up.

Establish set devotions within your family and make them special

One of the most efficacious devotions within the Roman Catholic Church is the First Friday and First Saturday devotions (see Appendix C). In Church-approved apparitions, Our Lord and Our Lady have requested that individuals go to church to receive the Eucharist on the first Friday and first Saturday of every month, as well as to go to Confession within a week of these special days. Make the First Friday/First Saturday devotions a staple of your family's prayer life. We add a special treat to make the children more motivated by going out for donuts after the First Saturday morning Mass. It has become an enjoyable tradition for our family, and is a gentle reminder of the need for all of us to attend monthly confession.

Another good family tradition to establish is May Day to give special honor to Our Lady. We give each child a candle and process around the home with a statue or image of Our Blessed Mother while singing or saying simple prayers.

Celebrate the sacraments by doing something special

Most people celebrate the Baptism of their children, but often other sacraments are overlooked. When a child makes his/her First Confession, First Holy Communion, and Confirmation, make these joyful family celebrations. Go out to eat or have a family party to truly celebrate the sacrament and make an impression upon the child regarding the special nature of the day.

Monitor children's television programming

This may seem obvious, but even seemingly harmless children's TV networks like The Disney Channel and Nickelodeon can carry some inappropriate shows. Preview each regular show first and make a list of shows that are definite "no-nos" in your home. Children will usually accept the boundaries that you set with little resistance, especially if you begin when they are very young.

Keep Christ in Christmas

Despite the secularization of this holy feast day, it is up to us as parents to keep the focus where it belongs. It's not wrong to allow the children to enjoy Santa Claus, but why not let the kids know that Santa was based on a real Catholic saint? Get a movie about the life of St. Nicholas (see Resource 12) and try to see and experience Santa as a way to remember this real and blessed saint. Remember the joy children have in experiencing their faith with the senses. Get an advent wreath with candles and light it nightly before dinner, meditating shortly before grace with prayers or booklets. Put up a Nativity Set and say evening prayers in front of it during Advent. One way to get little ones involved is to keep the figurines in a bag, then pull out one new figurine for the crèche every night before saying prayers and add it to the set. Get an advent calendar which allows the children to take turns opening up the daily "windows." Get one that centers around scripture passages and baby Jesus.

Dress up for Sunday Church

Despite the current trend in many parishes to dress casually for Sunday Mass, make it a habit from the earliest age to dress nicely for Church, particularly on Sunday. When children have established this habit from an early age, it will stick with them. It demonstrates and emphasizes a basic love and respect for Our Lord.

Have everyone participate in Lenten fasts

Even though Church law does not require abstaining from meat on Fridays during Lent for children under the age of 14, make this Lenten sacrifice a family activity. Even the youngest children can easily abstain from meat along with the rest of the family, and be taught valuable lessons in the need for simple sacrifices.

Teach children the value of voluntary, regular acts of mortification

Our Lady of Medjugorje has asked repeatedly for the past years to fast on bread and water on Wednesdays and Fridays. If we can't do this type of fast, She recommends offering up another chosen form of individual penance instead. We give up desserts every Wednesday and Friday throughout the year. This is a concept that even very young children can comprehend when put in simple terms: "Let's give our ice cream bar dessert to Jesus to have tonight instead of us, okay?" Such small acts of sacrifice, when done on a regular basis, will help build life-long habits of self-mortification.

Teach your children to establish devotion to particular saints and the holy angels

Choose a few specific saints for your family to pray to on a regular basis. St. Anthony is especially popular around our house when something is lost or misplaced. St. Michael the Archangel is another favorite. Let each child develop a devotion to his/her patron saint by wearing a medal of that saint or having a prayer card with the saint's picture displayed in the child's room. Also, help your children to develop an awareness of the holy angels, especially their own special guardian angel. Choose a name for each child's guardian angel to develop a more personal relationship. Say the guardian angel prayer every morning and every evening. Teach children to call upon their guardian angel in time of distress or fright.

Make visits to the Blessed Sacrament

Whether just passing by the Church to visit Jesus in the tabernacle, or making visits to Our Lord in Eucharistic Adoration, make short visits to Jesus with your children. An 18-month-old may only be able to stand a two minute visit, but these are wonderful opportunities to teach even young children about the True Presence of Our Blessed Lord in the Eucharist.

Develop a healthy awareness in your children of Hell and Satan

It's not recommended to frighten the children by overdoing it, but let your children know about the reality of Hell and the devil. Knowing and acknowledging these realities helps to explain much of the evil in our world today which children are constantly exposed to in the media and television. Even young children will have questions about why a mother could kill her own children, or some of the other particularly heinous crimes which make the headlines daily. Explaining the reality and existence of Satan and his influence in our world today can help children make some sense of it.

Don't be afraid to say grace as a family in public places

When going out to eat, don't let your family's habit of saying grace before meals be thrown out the window. Do not reveal shame or embarrassment to your children by being hesitant to do the Sign of the Cross and your normal grace prayer before meals, no matter where you are.

Bring religious books to church for younger children

If your very young children need to bring books to Church to help keep them occupied, make them religious in nature. There are many wonderful Bible stories and picture books which are available at any Catholic or Christian bookstore.

No matter where your children go to school, plan to "home school" them in religion

Even the best Catholic schools today may fail to adequately teach the children the fundamental rudiments of the Roman Catholic Faith which was available with the old Catechism programs (the *Baltimore Catechism*). Whether your kids are in Catholic schools or public schools, plan on most of the teaching regarding our faith being done by yourself at home. Don't depend on any school, even a Catholic one, to adequately instruct your children in all of the specific aspects and beliefs related to our faith. Plan to accept this challenge as one of the primary objectives of your vocation as mother.

Purchase Catholic videotapes for your children

There are a variety of wonderful animated Catholic videos available on the market today (see Resource 12). Take time to build up a library of good Catholic videos for your children to enjoy, and encourage them to watch them often.

Teach your children to make rosaries

The simple bead kits for rosary making can be acquired through several sources. Inexpensively priced rosary making kits may be purchased from: Our Lady's Rosary Makers, P.O. Box 37080, Louisville, KY 40233. Even very young children can enjoy making their own special rosary. Have them bring their special rosary to Mass and ask the priest to bless it. As children grow older and are more able to make the rosaries, consider making them for the poor and for foreign missions.

Discipline your children with the eyes of the Blessed Mother and Our Lord

Every parent needs to enforce discipline occasionally – whether it be with a screaming toddler, a stubborn five-year-old or an outspoken teen. It is important that parents take the necessary steps to discipline children for inappropriate behavior, but here's a little tip to help you to maintain a spirit of love when you discipline: imagine that Jesus or Mary is sitting right there in the room watching you admonish your child. Would you speak/behave any differently if Our Lord or Our Lady was actually sitting there observing you? I find this to be a sobering thought at times when I'm tempted to raise my voice, perhaps unnecessarily. Try it!

Teach your children the value of personal suffering

The old saying that we may have all heard from our moms while growing up and experiencing physical pain, "Offer it up!" still applies today! When children suffer the inevitable cuts, scrapes, and bruises, teach them the value of offering the pain up to Jesus as a personal sacrifice, or as a gift to Him. The idea of redemptive suffering is one that many adults don't quite understand, but children will comprehend it when you keep it simple. A simple prayer like, "Jesus, I give you this pain," is all you need to teach or remind your child to say when these opportunities arise.

Use correct terms when teaching children the fundamental truths of our Catholic Faith

Even though you may have to simplify explanations of terminology related to the Roman Catholic Faith (i.e., Purgatory, Reconciliation, Eucharist, Reparation), keep the vocabulary true. In other words, use the word "Purgatory," then explain in simple terms that it is a place of waiting to be completely cleansed of sin before entering Heaven. Even the youngest children will soon learn the proper terminology, and you can expand on the explanations as the child grows.

Celebrate Halloween as a Christian Holiday

Today Halloween has gained much notice as a "pagan holiday" and has even been connected with various demonic practices. Counteract this by celebrating this day as a time to remember the eve of All Saints Day as a day of reverence and respect for the communion of saints in Heaven. Instead of dressing up in frightening costumes which impress evil, like witches, devils, ghosts, and ghouls, try having your children dress as their favorite saint instead! We found that just adding a pair of large, majestic wings to a costume of sword and armour quickly transformed our son from a knight into St. Michael the Archangel! When he wore the costume to a Christian Church which was having an alternative celebration to "trick or treating," he got lots of interesting comments and questions. Many saints have characteristic dress which you can duplicate with a little fabric and lots of imagination. Use Halloween as a time to emphasize the wonderful idea of the communion of Saints, as well as a time to remember to pray for the Poor Souls in Purgatory.

Conclusion

Perhaps you have already heard of many of the simple ideas presented in this section for teaching the faith to our children. Possibly you grew up with a lot of these concepts, as I did. If not, it is my sincere hope that you will find some of the tips and hints easy to incorporate or modify for use in your own life as a Catholic mom. As mothers, we are entrusted with the most difficult, yet most important job in the world. God has entrusted the care of little souls to our guidance, instruction, love, and nurturing. It is our job as Catholic mothers to bring these young ones up to become Godly souls who will glorify Him some day in His Kingdom. There is no better or more crucial job in our world today.

RESOURCE LIST

Resource 1: The most wonderful rosary booklet I have found with gorgeous full-color pictures to accompany each mystery is ***Prayer of the Heart*** by Fr. Bob Wright. It's available for a donation through Apostolate of the Word, Sacred Heart League, Walls, Mississippi 38686, (601) 781-1360. Rosary audio tapes are available through The Riehle Foundation, P.O. Box 7, Milford OH 45150.

Resource 2: ***The Wonders of the Holy Name*** is a terrific little booklet that explains how just repeating the name of Jesus is a powerful and efficacious prayer. It is available through TAN Books, P.O. Box 424, Rockford, IL 61105.

Resource 3: Two wonderful books with meditations for Eucharistic Adoration are available through The Riehle Foundation (address above). The books are titled, ***An Hour With Jesus (Volume I*** and ***Volume II).***

Resource 4: An abundant supply of free, blessed Miraculous Medals may be obtained by sending a donation to: The Association of the Miraculous Medal, St. Mary's Seminary, 1811 W. Saint Joseph St., Perryville, MO 63775-1598.

Resource 5: **Catholic Household Blessings & Prayers** contains more information about house blessings and may be obtained for $9.95 plus postage from the United States Catholic Conference, Inc., (800)235-8722.

Resource 6: A great example of a "defend your faith" type of book is *Rome Sweet Home,* by Scott and Kimberly Hahn, published by Ignatius Press, and is available in most Catholic bookstores. Another book is called *Surprised by Truth,* also available through The Riehle Foundation.

Resource 7: *The Apostolate of Holy Motherhood* has been a faith turning point for mothers throughout the United States. It is a powerful book and will truly change your life and the way you look at being a mother. It may be obtained from: The Apostolate of Holy Motherhood, P.O. Box 227, Geneva, OH 44041.

Resource 8: A wonderful version of the computerized *Catechism of the Catholic Church* designed for children grades 3 - 7 is available through: Gannon University, Erie, PA 16541. The title of the series is **"Cybercat – Catalogue of Faith."**

Resource 9: There are some terrific Catholic sites to visit on the Internet (WWW). If you have a computer with Internet capacity, type in a search for the following sites. (URL addresses are not listed here because the Internet is an ever changing environment and some locations may have moved or closed by the time you read this book.) These are great places to start!

A) The Catholic Goldmine
B) The Catholic Mothers Internet Connection
C) Catholic Online On the Web
D) Christus Rex
E) Catholic Files
F) Catholic Information Center on the Internet
G) Catholic Resources on the Net
H) Catholic Links to Catholic Related Sites
I) Catholic City

Resource 10: The book needed to do the Total Consecration to Jesus and Mary is called *Preparation for Total Consecration according to St. Louis Marie de Montfort,* Montfort Publications, Bay Shore, NY 11706. It is available in many Catholic bookstores. Shorter versions of daily consecrations may be found in *The Gold Book of Prayers,* available through

The Riehle Foundation.

Resource 11: For how to say the ***Chaplet of Divine Mercy*** and other related information, contact: Marian Helpers, Eden Hill, Stockbridge, MA 01263.

Resource 12: Great children's animated Catholic videos can be obtained through CCC of America, 1-800-935-2222.

PRAYER LIST

Suggestions for morning and evening prayers:

Morning Consecration Prayers:

Consecration to the Sacred Heart of Jesus and Immaculate Heart of Mary

Sacred Heart of Jesus and Immaculate Heart of Mary, I give myself and my whole family entirely to You [here name each child and your husband], and to show our devotion to You this day, we consecrate to You our eyes, our ears, our mouths, our hearts, our whole beings without reserve. Wherefore, dear Mother and sweet Jesus, as we are Your own, guard us and keep us always as Your property and possession. Amen.

Angel of God Prayer

Angel of God, my guardian dear, to whom God's love commits me here, ever this day [or night] be at my side, to light and guard, to rule and guide. Amen.

Nighttime prayers for the Family Altar:

Prayer to St. Michael the Archangel

St. Michael the Archangel, defend us in battle, be our defense against the wickedness and snares of the devil. May God rebuke him, we humbly pray, and do you, O Prince of the Heavenly Host, by the divine Power of God, thrust into Hell Satan and all the other evil spirits, who wander through the world seeking the ruin of souls. Amen.

Fatima Prayer

Oh my God, I believe, I adore, I trust, and I love You. I beg pardon for all those who do not believe, do not adore, do not trust, and do not love You. Amen.

St. Gertrude's Prayer to release 1,000 souls from Purgatory

Oh my God, I offer Thee the most precious Blood of Thy Divine Son, Jesus, in union with all the Masses being offered throughout the world today, for the souls in Purgatory, for sinners everywhere, those in the Universal Church, and those in my own family.

Short Divine Mercy Prayer for Conversion

Oh Blood and Water, which gushed forth from the Heart of Jesus as a fountain of mercy for us, I trust in You.

ADDITIONAL RESOURCES FOR A HOME LIBRARY

Here is a list of recommended books for your library:

1) The *Catechism of the Catholic Church.* This is available at any Catholic bookstore and comes in hardback, soft cover, and even a small paperback version (my personal favorite!). No Catholic home should be without it! It is available through Doubleday Books, 1540 Broadway, New York, NY 10036.

2) *Pierced by a Sword* by Bud McFarlane, Jr. If you haven't read this one yet, prepare yourself! It is a heart-stopping fictional account of what might occur over the next few years as the many prophesies of Our Blessed Mother come to fulfillment. You will not be able to put it down! It is available for free, donations greatfully accepted. Send requests to: St. Jude Media, Box 26120, Fairview Park, OH 44126.

3) *Our Lady Teaches About Sacramentals and Blessed Objects* by Rev. Albert J. M. Shamon. This booklet gives you a great deal of in-depth

information about sacramentals and blessed objects, their history and tradition. It is available through The Riehle Foundation.

4) *Rome Sweet Home* by Scott and Kimberly Hahn. This is a wonderful account of how this very strong Protestant couple became converts to the Roman Catholic Faith. It is a great "defend your faith" kind of book. It is available in most Catholic bookstores. You can also acquire audio and video cassette tapes of the Hahns covering a wide range of Scripture and Catholic doctrine, as well as tapes by inspired Catholic speakers from: St. Joseph's Communication, Inc., P.O. Box 720, West Covina, CA 91793, 1-800-526-2151.

5) *The Final Hour* by Michael Brown. This is a terrific book that is available in most Catholic bookstores or through The Riehle Foundation. It gives a fascinating summary of many of the reported apparitions of Our Lady which are occurring throughout the world and what they may mean.

6) *Divine Mercy in my Soul — The Diary of Blessed Faustina*. Beautiful meditations to read and all necessary prayers and background information related to the Divine Mercy devotion. Available in most Catholic bookstores, or

from Marian Helpers, Eden Hill, Stockbridge, MA 01263.

7) ***Catholic Homeschooling: A Handbook for Parents*** by Mary Kay Clark. In this book, Dr. Clark supplies ideas about discipline, home management, socialization, Catholic teachings, and Catholic family life as they relate to Catholic home schooling. Available through TAN Books & Publishers, Inc., Box 424, Rockford, IL 61105.

8) ***Thoughts and Sayings of St. Margaret Mary.*** A beautiful little booklet with short and easy to read meditations taken from the inspired words of this wonderful saint. Available from TAN Books (address above).

9) ***The Holy Eucharist*** by St. Alphonsus de Liguori. This book is one of the definitive books written on and about the Holy Eucharist and has beautiful meditations for Eucharistic Adoration. Available through TAN Books.

10) ***A Catholic Handbook for Engaged and Newly Married Couples*** by Frederick W. Marks, Ph.D. This is a comprehensive study of the Church's teachings on marriage, offering advice on such topics as finances, recreation, and spirituality. From the Riehle Foundation.

11) *Draw Me – Catholic Prayers for Every Occasion in a Woman's Life* selected by Carmen Rojas. This beautiful prayer book has a variety of prayers taken from many sources conveniently listed under headings. Published by Servant Publications, P.O. Box 8617, Ann Arbor, MI 48107.

12) **Mini-Books by Mother Angelica**. This is a fantastic series of booklets and leaflets with meditations on a wide range of topics – from *Spiritual Hangovers* to *Praying into Prayer*. A complete listing of all of her books is available through EWTN Catholic Publisher, 5817 Old Leeds Rd., Irondale, AL 35210.

13) *Rosary Meditations from Mother Teresa of Calcutta* by Fr. Martin Lucia, M.S.S. These powerful rosary meditations are Eucharistic in nature and meant to be read while reciting the Rosary at Eucharistic Adoration. Available through Apostolate of Perpetual Adoration, P.O. Box 46502, Mt. Clemens, MI 48046-6502.

14) *Crossing the Threshold of Hope* by His Holiness John Paul II. This bestseller is available through any secular or Catholic bookstore. It is a priceless array of essays written by the Pope to answer many people's most common questions about the Faith.

15) *A Popular Guide Based on the Catechism of the Catholic Church – The Faith* by John Hardon, S.J. This is a wonderful compliment-ary commentary on the *Catechism* in question and answer format, much like the old *Baltimore Catechism*. Available from Servant Publications.

16) *Modern Saints – Their Lives and Faces, Vol. 1 & 2,* by Ann Ball. These books will help you and your family become more familiar with the wonderful communion of saints that are awaiting our requests for their prayerful intervention. It is available from TAN Books.

17) *Our Sunday Visitor's Catholic Encyclo-pedia* ed. by Fr. Peter Stravinskas, Ph.D., S.T.L. This is rich in Scripture, steeped in canon law, and comprehensive. Available through Our Sunday Visitor Publishing Division, Hunting-ton, 200 Noll Plaza, IN 46750.

BOOKS FOR CHILDREN

1) **The Arch Book Bible Library** is a whole series of children's stories from both the Old and New Testaments. Available at many Catholic bookstores.

2) **Individual Lives of the Saints** books by Mary Fabyan Windeatt. This is a series of twenty books written about the most famous saints for young people ages 10 and up. It includes: St. Benedict, St. Catherine of Sienna, St. Théresè of Liseux, St. Margaret Mary, among others. It is available from TAN Books.

3) **St. Joseph Picture Books – Treasury of the Catholic Faith.** This series of books has topics ranging from the angels to stories from the Bible. They are available wherever Catholic books are sold and through the Catholic Book Publishing Corp., 77 West End Rd., Totowa, NJ 07512.

4) *Just You & Jesus.* Prayers and meditations written specifically for anyone 12 to 17 years of age. It includes questions important to today's youth. Available from The Riehle Foundation.

5) *An Introduction to the Promise of St. Joseph: The Challenge of Chastity* by Fr. Bartholomew O'Brien. Inspires hope for any young person struggling to remain pure or regain his or her innocence in a difficult world. Available through The Riehle Foundation.

APPENDIX A

Sacramental Resources

Unless otherwise noted, you can acquire most through Catholic bookstores or mail order places.

Here is a list of various sacramentals you may wish to acquire for your home:

1) **The Scapular**: This is essential for all members in your family to wear. Even children should begin wearing them after being enrolled (usually after making their First Holy Communion). Wearing one is a little bothersome at first, but read about the wonderful promises attached to wearing one, and you will soon find it is not so tough to keep it on.

2) **Blessed Rosaries**: Keep rosaries all over your house, then you'll always have one handy when you may have a few minutes to squeeze in a few decades. Get them blessed by a priest.

3) **Medals**: There are lots of blessed medals to have around your home. The best ones are Miraculous medals and/or St. Benedict medals, which should be placed above each doorway of

your home for safety and protection. You can order blessed St. Benedict medals (which have the exorcism blessing on them) for 15¢ each from: The Benedictine Mission House, P.O. Box 528, Schuyler, NE 68661-0528. To order beautiful medals of your favorite saints at a very reasonable price by mail order contact: J.M.J. Products, 15581 W. 141 St., Olathe, KS 66062. Toll free (888) 350-8127.
www. totallycatholic. com

4) **Blessed Crucifixes**: Every Catholic home should have at least one prominently displayed. It's nice if you could acquire small ones to have in everyone's individual room.

5) **Pictures/Images of Our Lady, Our Lord, and the Saints**: These are wonderful to have around your home to remind you to pray throughout your busy days. Most people keep pictures of their own family members prominently displayed throughout their homes because they love them. Why not do the same for Our Lord and Our Lady?

6) **Blessed Salt**: This is a very powerful sacramental and protection against evil. It is one of the oldest sacramentals of our Church, but has just recently received renewed interest. It is used like holy water, and may be ingested

in food (for healing) or sprinkled around your home, especially at all doorways and entryways, for protection. Any priest can bless any amount of salt you bring to him with the standard Roman Ritual Blessing for salt. If your priest doesn't know it, here it is: "Almighty God, we ask you to bless this salt, as once you blessed the salt scattered over the water by the prophet Elisha. Wherever this salt (and water) is sprinkled, drive away the power of evil, and protect us always by the presence of your Holy Spirit. Grant this through Christ our Lord. Amen." You may receive a pamphlet explaining the history and use of blessed salt along with this blessing prayer from: Fr. John Hampsch, C.M.F., Claretian Tape Ministry, P.O. Box 19100, Los Angeles, CA 90019.

7) **Holy Water**: Keep it around in abundance and use it often. Put it in a squirt bottle (clearly marked) and use it to squirt the different rooms of your home. Put up a holy water font in your home so your family members can bless themselves with holy water before going to bed or upon rising in the morning. You can order blessed Holy Water from Lourdes for a donation from: Missionary Oblates of Mary Immaculate, National Shrine of Our Lady of the Snows, 442 S. DeMazenod Dr., Belleville, IL 62223. Phone 1-618-397-6700.

8) **Blessed Candles**: Have these on your family altar to light at night when saying evening prayers. Kids especially love candles! Any votive candle that you purchase should be blessed by a priest.

9) **Sacred Heart Badge**: All moms should wear one, according to Our Blessed Mother in messages she gave to a young midwestern mother. It's a small badge that you can pin to the inside of your clothing with an invocation to Our Lord and an image of the Sacred Heart.

10) **Blessed Holy Cards**: Get holy cards at any Catholic bookstore of your favorite saints or your children's patron saints, and have them blessed by a priest. You can also mail order full-color laminated holy cards very reasonably priced through J.M.J. Products, 15581 W. 141 St., Olathe, KS 66062. Toll Free (888) 350-8127 www.totallycatholic.com

11) **Agnus Dei**: This is a sacramental made of pure, white, virgin wax, blessed by Our Holy Father at certain seasons. Those who carry or venerate this are promised protection from tempests, lightning, fire, water, malice of demons and adversity, pestilence, sickness and sudden death. It comes in the form of a small

piece of pressed wax, about the size of a coin, in some sort of pouch. You can carry it with you, or put it in your purse, etc. This sacramental, along with the Little Sachet (mentioned below) are both available for a $5.00 donation from: Discalced Carmelite Nuns, 73530 River Rd., Covington, LA 70435-2206.

12) **The Little Sachet of the Adorable Name of Jesus:** A small cloth piece meant to excite confidence when calling on of the Adorable name of Jesus. Available through the Discalced Carmelite Nuns (see address above).

APPENDIX B

Explanation of Indulgences

The following is an explanation of Indulgences as taken from The *Catechism of the Catholic Church,* Doubleday Books, 1540 Broadway, New York, NY 10036, Copyright 1994.

1471. Indulgences: The doctrine and practice of indulgences in the Church are closely linked to the affects of the sacrament of Penance. An indulgence is the remission before God of the temporal punishment due to sins whose guilt has already been forgiven, which the faithful Christian who is duly disposed gains under certain prescribed conditions through the action of the Church which, as the minister of redemption, dispenses and applies with authority the treasury of the satisfactions of Christ and the saints. An indulgence is partial or plenary according as it removes either part or all of the temporal punishment due to sin. Indulgences may be applied to the living or the dead.

APPENDIX C

Explanation of First Friday and First Saturday Devotions

The First Friday devotions was established based on revelations from Our Lord as given to St. Margaret Mary Alocoque for those devoted to the Sacred Heart of Jesus. Traditionally this devotion consists of receiving Holy Communion on nine consecutive first Fridays of the month to serve as an act of reparation for the outrages and sacrileges committed against the Sacred Heart of Jesus. Among Our Lord's 12 Promises to St. Margaret Mary was, *"I promise thee, in the exceeding great mercy of My Heart, that its all-powerful love will grant to all those who will receive Holy Communion on nine consecutive first Fridays of the month, the grace of final repentance, not dying in My disfavor, and without receiving their sacraments, My divine Heart becoming their assured refuge at the last moment."*

Regarding First Saturdays: The Blessed Mother revealed the following promise to Sr. Lucia of the Immaculate Heart, a Fatima visionary: *"Have compassion on the Heart of your most Holy Mother, covered with thorns, with which ungrateful men pierce it at every moment, and there is no one to make an act of reparation to remove them. Look, my daughter, at my Heart surrounded with thorns with which ungrateful men pierce me at every moment by their blasphemies and ingratitude. You at least try to console me, and say that I promise to assist at the hour of death, with the graces necessary for salvation, all those who, on the first Saturday of five consecutive months, shall confess, receive Holy Communion, recite five decades of the Rosary, and keep me company for fifteen minutes while meditating on the fifteen mysteries of the Rosary, with the intention of making reparation to me."* The act of confession may be made any time during the eight days prior to or after the First Saturday.

APPENDIX D

Catholic Magazines and Periodicals

Addresses and subscription rates are accurate as of September 1998. Information regarding pricing and acquiring materials presented throughout the book is subject to change.

The Catholic Answer
(Our Sunday Visitor Publishing Co.)
200 Noll Plaza
Huntington, IN 46750
Telephone: (800) 348-2440
Frequency: 6 per year. Cost: $18.00 per year.
Answers questions about the Catholic faith. Edited by Fr. Peter Stravinskas. It contains articles plus a lengthy Catholic Q&A section.

Catholic Digest
P.O. Box 51551
Boulder, CO 80322-1551
Telephone: (303) 604-0765
Frequency: Monthly. Cost: $19.95 per year.
Basically a *Reader's Digest* for Catholics. Contains humor, columns, and reprints from Catholic books and periodicals.

Catholic Heritage
200 Noll Plaza
Huntington, IN 46750
Telephone: (800) 348-2440
Frequency: 6 per year. Cost: $18.00 per year.
Captivating, colorful depictions of the treasures of Catholicism – saints, icons, relics, shrines, the Vatican and more!

The Catholic Parent
200 Noll Plaza
Huntington, IN 46750-4304
Telephone: (219) 356-8400
Frequency: 6 per year. Cost: $18.00 per year.
Excellent articles of interest to parents raising Catholic kids in today's secular world.

The Catholic World Report
Subscription Dept.
P.O. Box 591300
San Francisco, CA 94159-1300
Telephone: (800) 651-1531
Frequency: 11 per year. Cost: $39.95 per year.
International news magazine with informative articles on current topics. (Price listed is for new subscribers.)

Canticle

Subscription Department
3050 Gap Knob Road
New Hope, KY 40052
Telephone: (888) 708-0813

Frequency: 6 per year. Cost: $26.95 per year.
A journal of the authentic Catholic woman which emphasizes traditional perspectives on a variety of timely topics.

Inside the Vatican

Subscription Department
3050 Gap Knob Road
New Hope, KY 40052

Telephone: (800) 789-9494
Frequency: 10 per year. Cost: $39.95 per year.
With editorial offices in Rome, Italy, this periodical presents news from the Vatican and addresses current controversies and topics of debate within the Church.

My Daily Visitor

200 Noll Plaza
Huntington, IN 46750

Telephone: (800) 348-2440
Frequency: 6 per year. Cost: $9.95 per year.
Daily readings and reflections which promote a refreshing breath of inspiration.

National Catholic Register

P.O. Box 373

Mt. Morris, IL 61054-0373

Telephone: (800) 421-3230

Frequency: Weekly. Cost: $49.95 per year.

Surveys national and international news of Catholic interest, politics, devotions, Scripture, prayer, etc. Conservative, but not traditionalist; positive in approach.

New Covenant

200 Noll Plaza

Huntington, IN 46750

Telephone: (800) 348-2440

Frequency: 12 per year. Cost: $18.00 per year.

Marriage, family life, parish renewal. Columnists include Ralph Martin, Fr. Michael Scanlan, Peter Kreeft. National magazine for charismatic renewal.

Origins

Catholic News Service

3211 Fourth St. NE

Washington, DC 20017

Telephone: (202) 541-3291

Frequency: Weekly. Cost: $99.00 per year.

"Invaluable." Original sources for all official Church documents, pastoral letters, etc. of both the US bishops as well as Vatican and the Pope.

Our Sunday Visitor

200 Noll Plaza
Huntington, IN 46750

Telephone: (800) 348-2440
Frequency: Weekly. Cost: $29.95 per year.
Terrific weekly features and up-to-date news from a Catholic perspective.

The Pope Speaks

200 Noll Plaza
Huntington, IN 46750

Telephone: (800) 348-2440
Frequency: 6 per year. Cost: $19.95 per year.
A chronical of addresses, sermons, speeches, and homilies given by the Pope.

Share the Word

PCNEA
3031 Fourth St. N.E.
Washington, DC 20017

Telephone: (202) 832-5022
Frequency: Bi-Monthly. Cost: $18.00 per year.
The nation's largest Catholic Bible study and sharing program. Focuses on the Sunday Lectionary readings. A reliable and easy to understand resource for liturgy groups, lector training, etc.

This Rock

Catholic Answers
P.O. Box 17490
San Diego, CA 92177

Telephone: (888) 291-8000
Frequency: Monthly. Cost: $29.95 per year.
Excellent magazine of Catholic evangelization and apologetics. Edited by Karl Keating, with features including "The Fathers Know Best" (patristics). Highly recommended.

Appendix E

Magazines and Materials for Youth

My Friend Magazine

50 St. Paul Ave.
Boston, MA 02130-3491

Telephone: (800) 876-4463
Frequency: 10 per year. Cost: $18.00 per year.
A magazine for children ages 6 - 12.

Hearts Aflame

The Blue Army
P.O. Box 976
Washington, NJ 07882-0976

Telephone: (908) 213-2223
Frequency: Quarterly. Cost: $5.00 per year.
This magazine is extremely orthodox, and rich in a variety of subjects related to the faith.

You!

29963 Mulholland Hwy.
Agoura Hills, CA 91301

Telephone: (818) 991-1813
Frequency: 10 per year. Cost: $19.95 per year.
Examines pop culture and difficult moral topics in light of the Catholic faith. For teenagers. Very good!

Holy Traders *(high quality Saints Trading Cards)*

J.M.J. Productions
15581 W. 141 St
Olathe, KS 66062

Telephone: (888) 350-8127
www.totallycatholic.com
Each set costs $7.95.
These are similar to baseball cards. They are designed for children in elementary school. There are two sets currently available. Set 1 has 30 cards, while Set 2 has 24 cards.

The National Catholic Insurgent

135 Olympia Ave.
North Providence, RI 02911

Telephone (401) 231-6743
A new national Catholic high school newspaper for teens, 9-18.

Divinity

Telephone (800) 669-9200

1) *The Catholic Quiz Flip Books* 200 questions and answers on Catechism, K-9th grade.
2) *The Catholic Challenge* Computer game with 2,000 questions on Catechism for all ages.
3) *The Catholic Challenge Bible Game on CD-ROM* Over 2,000 questions & answers for learning Sacred Scripture.

THE RIEHLE FOUNDATION . . .

The Riehle Foundation is a non-profit, tax-exempt, charitable organization that exists to produce and/or distribute Catholic material to anyone, anywhere.

The Foundation is dedicated to the Mother of God and her role in the salvation of mankind. We believe that this role has not diminished in our time, but, on the contrary has become all the more apparent in this the era of Mary as recognized by Pope John Paul II, whom we strongly support.

During the past nine years the foundation has distributed over four million books, films, rosaries, bibles, etc. to individuals, parishes, and organizations all over the world. Additionally, the foundation sends materials to missions and parishes in a dozen foreign countries.

Donations forwarded to The Riehle Foundation for the materials distributed provide our sole support. We appreciate your assistance, and request your prayers.

IN THE SERVICE OF JESUS AND MARY

All for the honor and glory of God!

The Riehle Foundation

P.O. Box 7

Milford, OH 45150

Other Titles Available for Families

Contact The Riehle Foundation

The Ten Commandments of God

by Rev. Albert J.M. Shamon. Contains common sense explanations as to why God gifted us with these guides for life and how they are to be lived today.

Fire from Above

by René Kieda. A truly gripping story for all who struggle with drugs, alcohol and crime. This is a book of hope especially for our youth or anyone tempted to despair.

Behind the Mass

by Rev. J.M. Shamon. An excellent book which explores the depth of meaning underlying the Mass.

Our Lady Says: Monthly Confession Remedy for the West

by Rev. Albert J.M. Shamon. A defense in clear-cut language of the purpose and importance of this often misunderstood sacrament.

Firepower Through Confirmation

by Rev. Albert J.M. Shamon. A teaching guide about Confirmation and the Holy Spirit which utilizes the Bible. Excellent activities!

Building A Legacy of Love

by Mary Ann Kuharski. A book for parents, grandparents and care givers with guidelines for raising children and bolstering family life.

The Riehle Foundation
P.O. Box 7
Milford, OH 45150 USA